Erased Verses

A Reflective Connection Collection

Lauren Leibly

Made with ❤ on the BookLeaf Publishing Platform
www.bookleafpub.in
www.bookleafpub.com

Dedication

To those who have felt the depths of pain, navigated the complexities of love, and faced the challenges of connection, and to those who silently battle depression—this collection is for you. May these words offer you solace, understanding, and a reminder that you are never alone. Your strength and resilience are a constant source of inspiration, and I hope these poems provide a moment of comfort and reflection on your journey.

With love,
Lauren

Preface

Words have always held profound meaning for me. From childhood, I've been captivated by language and the way it shapes our connections with others. In "Erased Verses," I've poured my heart into verses that reflect my own experiences with pain, love, connection, and the struggle with depression.

This collection is not just a random assortment of poems; it is a reflection of my journey through the complex layers of emotion. Each line is crafted with the hope that it resonates with those who have felt the weight of existence or faced their own struggles with connection.

Within these pages, you'll find the raw essence of love, the depth of pain, and a continuous quest to understand life's mysteries. My hope is that these poems offer you a space to feel, reflect, and find solace, knowing you are not alone.

Acknowledgements

I want to give a huge shoutout to my great friend, Maria Stant. Without her, I might be too insane to write this. You have been my rock, not only with my writing but in all the grand life questions. I never feel judged by you. I can give you all my words, scattered and messy, and you will love me just the same. This kind of love is hard to come by, and for that, I am so very thankful.

I would also like to extend my gratitude to anyone who has taken the time to preview my work. Your insights and feedback have been so helpful and do not go unnoticed.

Last but not least, I'd like to thank my readers. You are the reason I decided to publish my collection of poetry.

1. The Call of the Void

The
Heavens
Enclose

Crashing waves from below, they call,
Abyss beckons me to fall.
Lured to death by my despair,
Last words hanging in the air.

Off the cliff—
Freeing my soul.

This
Hell
Ends.

Vastness swallows, my breath shallows,
Over the ledge, my feet to the edge.
In the stillness, I pause,
Destiny's silent, no applause.

Description:

This acrostic poem, "The Call of the Void," uses the first letters of each line to spell out a powerful message. It evokes a sense of impending doom and existential reflection as the narrator stands at the edge of a cliff, contemplating the abyss. The vivid imagery and stark contrasts between despair and the calm of the void create a haunting exploration of the allure and finality of surrender.

Reflection Questions:

How do the images of the cliff and the abyss in the poem relate to any feelings of uncertainty or challenge you might have faced? Can you think of a time when you felt on the edge of making a big decision?

The poem describes a moment of letting go and finding freedom. Have you ever experienced a situation where you had to let go of something to move forward? What helped you through that process?

The poem contrasts feelings of overwhelming pressure with moments of calm. Have you ever felt a mix of

strong emotions and quiet moments at the same time?
How did you handle those feelings?

2. Fleeting Glimmers

They say happiness comes naturally,
That a flip of a switch can turn sad to glad,
And advise us not to be mad.
But for some, it's not so clear,
It drives us mad, this unseen fear.
They don't understand why sadness dwells,
Unaware of its wicked spells.

They say happiness is ours to find,
Yet, often, we're left behind.
Thrown to the wolves, on nights so cold,

When all we need is a hand to hold.
"Please grab on tight, don't let go,"
We cry out in the dark, seeking the glow.
But the hand we reach for is so cold,

With no warmth, no one to hold.
So we stretch into the unknown,
One is both born and dies alone.

But in the fleeting moments between,
Could we hold each other?
Share in what's unseen?

If only for a moment, can we feel
The warmth of light that seems so unreal?
Maybe this could help us heal,

And in that touch, so brief but kind,
Find the glimmer of joy, lost in our mind.

Description:

This poem explores the complex and often misunderstood nature of happiness. It contrasts the simplistic notion that happiness should come easily with the reality of persistent sadness and the search for genuine connection. The poem reflects on the difficulty of finding solace and warmth in moments of darkness and the fleeting but significant impact of human connection in our lives.

Reflection Questions:

How do you relate to the idea that happiness should come easily versus the reality of struggling with sadness? Have you ever felt pressure to be happy despite ongoing challenges?

The poem speaks about reaching out for support and finding it lacking. Reflect on a time when you sought comfort or connection but felt it was not available. How did that experience affect you?

The poem suggests that brief moments of warmth and connection can be healing. Can you recall a small, meaningful interaction that brought you comfort or joy during a difficult time? How did it impact you?

3. Heart Fortress

I catch you in my gaze,
But you slip away, a leaf in the breeze.
I hold tight, but you sift like sand,
Leaving me frozen in winter's cold hand.

An eerie symphony fills my mind,
Silent screams keep me confined.
Each time I pry, hope fades and dies,
Stirring my soul with muted cries.

Did I misstep? I just wanted to be near,
Doubt's fiery breath, burns my ear,
I say it's okay, but the truth is clear—
This was never about me; it's only your fear.

You wear a thousand faces, blend with the masses,
But never let feelings trace your glasses.
A million connections, no true embrace,
Your heart is a fortress, shielded in place.

I hear your laughter, watch you talk,
But it's all surface, a shallow walk.
Afraid to dive in, to stir up the deep,
You pull away, your secrets to keep.

I wanted more, but you stayed apart.
In others, I found those who shared their hearts.
In them, I discovered the strength to be free,
No longer bound by what you couldn't see.

Now I let go, no more chasing your door—
I'm shattered but sure, I deserve more.
Your guarded heart, distant yet bold,
Was never mine to have or unfold.

Description:

This poem delves into the pain of trying to connect with someone who remains emotionally distant and inaccessible. It explores the frustration of reaching out and finding that the person remains guarded and unresponsive, despite the narrator's efforts. The poem captures the transition from longing and disappointment to the realization of self-worth and the decision to move on.

Reflection Questions:

How do you relate to the feeling of reaching out to someone who remains emotionally distant? Can you recall a time when you felt a strong desire to connect but faced barriers?

The poem describes a shift from frustration to self-realization and letting go. Reflect on a situation where you had to move on from a relationship or connection that was unfulfilling. How did you come to that decision?

The poem contrasts genuine connection with superficial interactions. How do you differentiate between meaningful relationships and those that feel shallow or unsatisfying? What qualities do you look for in a true connection?

4. Love Truly

Starry-eyed teenage dreams,
We tore each other apart at the seams.

New lovers with passion undefined,
Certain only of the spark when our bodies entwined.

Soon, our words turned to daggers, patience betrayed—
Is this how true love is made?

We drifted apart to rediscover our hearts,
Wondering if this was where our story starts.

We broke up, doubts running deep,
Yet reunited, with promises to keep.

Years flowed by, and children came,
Yet love's true yearning stayed the same.

Beneath the surface, we lingered as teens,
Lost in the dream of what love truly means.

Time etched lines on our aging faces,
While our views on love found different places.

We ponder and sigh at love's distant call,
A wave that rises only to fall.

Perhaps in our journey, we might find
What love truly is—and how it's defined.

Description:

This poem reflects on the evolving nature of love through the journey of two individuals who started as passionate young lovers. It captures their tumultuous relationship, the challenges of growing up together, and the shifting perceptions of love as they age. The poem explores the transition from youthful idealism to the complex realities of a long-term relationship, pondering what true love means over time.

Reflection Questions:

How do you relate to the idea of love evolving from passionate beginnings to a more complex and mature understanding? Have you experienced changes in your own view of love over time?

The poem speaks about breaking up and reuniting with promises to keep. Reflect on a time when you or someone you know experienced a similar pattern in a relationship. How did that impact your perception of love and commitment?

As the poem explores the differences between youthful dreams and the reality of aging, how do you think your own experiences have shaped your understanding of what love truly is? What has helped you redefine or reaffirm your beliefs about love?

5. Unmasked Oddity

You said you were weird—
so was I.
Together, we dropped the charade,
let our oddness align.

A bond we formed—so rare, so true,
Two misfits in sync, a perfect two.
But then came the shift, the blame fell on me,
And suddenly, all I knew of us was untrue.

The person I knew
slipped out of sight,
as our world unraveled
with all its might.

I still miss that spark,
the strange, wild flicker of you,
the one who cared,
the real, true you.
Now, everything's cooled,

our flame snuffed out,
and I wander the dark,
lost, misplaced, cast about.

I still think of you,
the one who walked through
only to change.
Two oddballs once perfectly matched,
now drifting apart
with no stitch to patch.

**The mask returns,
heavy on my face—
it was you who let me take it off,
and now, it's mine alone to embrace.**

Wherever you are,
I hope you're free.
As for me,
I'll own this weirdness—
fully, finally, me.

Description:

This poem explores the emotional fallout of a friendship
that once thrived on shared uniqueness and mutual
understanding. It reflects on the deep connection that

existed between two "weird" individuals who supported each other's authentic selves. As the relationship deteriorates and one friend accuses the other of insanity, the poem delves into the pain of losing that special bond and the struggle to reconcile with the changed dynamic. Ultimately, it's a contemplation of self-preservation and acceptance amidst the loss.

Reflection Questions:

How do you relate to the experience of finding and losing a deep connection with someone who understood and accepted you for who you are? Have you had a friendship where you felt a strong sense of shared identity that later changed?

The poem describes a shift from mutual understanding to being labeled as "insane." Reflect on a time when you felt misunderstood or unfairly judged by someone you were close to. How did that experience affect you?

The poem ends with the speaker choosing to stay true to themselves despite the loss of the friendship. How do you handle maintaining your identity when relationships or connections change? What strategies help you stay authentic to yourself?

6. Echoes of the Playground

In the playground's dusty haze,
Old wounds rise, fiercely ablaze.

An angry woman sparks a match,
With the biggest bully of the batch.

She shoves him with a tongue of tales,
Scripting scenes that make her wail.

He claims he can't recall,
But her memories stand tall.

A sincere sorry spills from his lips,
Now a man with earnest grips.

He confesses his own childhood hurt,
Once unnoticed, now alert.

She wrestles with this deep soul sore,
Forgiveness waiting at the door.

Contemplating his heartfelt plea,
She lights a path to set her free.

Though scars remain, etched and raw,
She embraces the change she saw.

Not forgetting, but slowly releasing
All the hate that she'd been keeping.

For some, apologies never arrive,
But she walks away, her spirit revived.

The boy who once caused her so much strife,
Has transformed and changed his whole life.

Description:

This poem portrays a woman confronting a former bully from her childhood. It depicts her emotional struggle as she confronts the past pain and the bully's subsequent apology. The poem captures her journey from anger and hurt to a place of forgiveness and personal growth, reflecting on how both the bully and the woman have changed over time. It highlights the complexities of forgiveness and the impact of acknowledging and releasing long-held grievances.

Reflection Questions:

How do you relate to the process of confronting past wounds and dealing with unresolved emotions? Have you experienced a situation where you had to address old grievances or confront someone from your past?

The poem explores the theme of forgiveness and its challenges. Reflect on a time when someone apologized for a past hurt. How did their apology affect you, and how did it influence your feelings towards them?

The woman in the poem moves from anger to forgiveness. How do you manage the process of letting go of past grievances and embracing personal growth? What steps do you take to release negative emotions and find peace?

7. Fading Tides

What's your favorite color? Mine is blue—
Is it yours, too?
Look, we're wearing matching shoes, a perfect pair,
Building sandcastles without a care.

We chased the waves, laughed at their roar,
But now our bond feels uncertain, unsure.
The tide has turned, our paths have diverged,
In the surf, where our words once emerged.

We talked of dreams and futures bright,
Now it's politics and endless spite.
I yearn for the peace we once knew,
This growing rift feels all too true.

Our friendship, once pure and kind,
Now drifts apart, leaving us behind.
I'm sorry, but I must move on—
This isn't the bond I once relied upon.

What we had was real and true,
But sometimes friends drift and come unglued.
I need to grow, and so must you—
It's time to let go and start anew.

Description:

This poem reflects on the changing nature of a friendship as shared experiences and dreams give way to growing differences and conflicts. Through imagery of past joys like matching outfits and carefree beach days, it contrasts with the present discord marked by disagreements and political differences. The poem conveys a bittersweet farewell as the speaker acknowledges the need to move on from a once-cherished bond that no longer aligns with their needs.

Reflection Questions:

How have your own friendships evolved over time, and what role do changing interests or values play in these shifts?

When faced with growing differences in a relationship, how do you determine whether to address the issues or let the bond naturally fade?

What are some ways to preserve meaningful connections
even as circumstances and personal growth lead to
change?

8. Silver Whispers

I panic, grab the bottle of dye,
Catching a shimmer in the corner of my eye.
Silver strands weave through my hair,
Time's threads appear—I wasn't aware.
I'm too young for these lines to show.

I smear on potions and gleaming creams,
Yet the change isn't quite what it seems.
A simple truth soon becomes clear—
I can't rewind what's already here.
Youth slipped through my fingers like cool rain,
Blooming into lessons, not learned in vain.

Whispers of truth softly emerge,
In the mirror's reflection, I observe—
It's not about how I look, but who I've become.
Silver whispers secrets long whirled,
Of moments missed in a fleeting world.

Each crease and fold maps the way,

Etched by paths where I've long strayed.
More than a mask that time can strip away,
With each year, old fears fall away.
It's who I am, not just how I display.

Time's a river, fierce and swift,
Its waters carve and also lift—
What's left behind feels strangely light.
A silver thread, unspun,
Where grace is found as days are done.

I swim with life, let go, and flow—
Embracing all that unfolds.

Description:

This poem reflects on the passage of time and the acceptance of aging. Through vivid imagery of silver strands and evolving lessons, it explores how youth and its fleeting nature give way to wisdom and self-discovery. The poem reveals that true beauty and value lie not in appearances but in the person we become over time. It celebrates the journey of letting go and embracing each moment with grace.

Reflective Questions:

How do you perceive the changes that come with aging?

Are there aspects of yourself that you struggle to accept, and how might embracing these changes shift your perspective?

What lessons have you learned from the passage of time that have reshaped your understanding of who you are? How do these lessons influence your daily life and decisions?

In what ways do you find beauty and value in the process of growing older? How can you shift your focus from external appearances to the inner qualities that define you?

9. Blood vs. Water

Blood is thicker than water,
But water breathes life, just as blood does.

In streams flow healing currents bright,
Though calm, their depths can hide the fight.
In blood, fierce bonds may often form,
Yet betrayal waits beneath the norm.

Oceans rage, both fierce and mild—
A quiet storm, both wild and styled.
And in the bonds we choose to keep,
Love runs as deep as blood can seep.

For sometimes friends stretch oceans wide,
Their waters hold when blood runs dry.
With hands that lift and hearts that guide,
They show the strength where waters rise.

Description:

This poem explores the relationship between blood (family) and water (friendship), using metaphors of streams and oceans to illustrate the strengths and complexities of both. It reflects on how familial bonds and friendships can be equally profound and supportive, emphasizing that true family can be found in the friends who stand by us.

Reflective Questions:

How do you experience the balance between the support of your family and the support of your friends in your own life?

Can you recall a time when a friend's support felt as strong or stronger than that of a family member?

In what ways do you think the depth of friendship can mirror or even surpass the bonds of blood relationships?

10. Resilient Grace

I've never touched a drug that's made
My mind decay or spirit fade—
I choose a path where light remains,
Untouched by poison coursing veins.

Not a powder, not a line
Can steal my strength or cloud my mind—
I stand unbroken, clear, and free,
Refusing chains that silence me.

Not a needle, not a high
Can strip the hope that helps me fly—
I rise above the darkest night,
Embracing dawn, embracing light.

A pill has never held my will
Or bent my dreams to lies that kill—
I find my peace in open skies,
Not in the haze where true self dies.

I've never touched the deadly dust,
Where fentanyl betrays all trust—
I walk a path where life prevails,
Beyond the reach of tragic tales.

I thank God those have never crossed my path,
It's only luck that spared me wrath—
A twist of fate, a guarded line,
That kept me safe from ruin's sign.

But if I had, would I be deemed as flawed?
Would you see me as a soul outlawed?
Would shadows drift me to a place of woe,
In a life where grace feels far from home?

Maybe it's those who've faced death's door
Who grasp love and war's core—
For they've braved the trials of pain,
And found the strength to rise again.

So next time you see a soul so broke,
Don't judge too quickly or revoke—
Their wounds may tell of battles fought,
And the strength from lessons taught.

Just be grateful you weren't steered that way,
For much of our fortune is luck's sway—

A delicate dance of fate and chance,
Guiding us clear from a dark trance.

Description:

"Resilient Grace" is a poignant exploration of strength and self-preservation amidst the temptation and peril of addiction. The poem reflects on the choice to remain untouched by destructive substances and acknowledges the role of luck and fate in navigating life's challenges. Through a journey of self-awareness and empathy, it delves into the struggle of maintaining integrity and the deep understanding of those who have faced their own trials.

Reflective Questions:

How do personal choices and external factors shape our path, and how do they influence our perception of those who struggle with addiction?

In what ways can empathy and understanding help us support others who are battling their own challenges, and how can this perspective impact our judgments?

What does it mean to find grace and strength in the face

of adversity, and how can acknowledging the role of luck
and fate help us navigate our own journeys?

11. Purest Me

You say I'm emotional,
Like a bipolar nightmare.
It can be true sometimes—
My emotions do rule.
When I'm joyful, it's pure glee;
When I'm angry, I'm really mean.
I wear my heart on my sleeve,
Swinging between extremes.

But you are my daylight all the time,
Even when you make my eyes run dry.
I can't stay mad when you're around;
Your warmth melts my stubborn frown.
In your presence, my storms subside;
The tempest in me begins to hide.
You bring calm to my turbulent sea;
Your love is my sanctuary.

I want you to have the purest me,
Unfiltered and sincere,

Every part of me, raw and true,
Shared with no pretense or fear.
In your gaze, I feel safe,
To show my complete, unguarded self.
For you, I'll strive to be my best;
In your embrace, I find my rest.

Description:

This poem explores the speaker's emotional intensity and vulnerability within a relationship. It depicts the highs and lows of their emotions, likening them to a "bipolar nightmare" yet acknowledging the grounding influence of their partner. The speaker contrasts their fluctuating emotions with the constant support and calming presence of their loved one, highlighting a deep sense of security and acceptance in their relationship.

Reflective Questions:

How do you relate to the experience of having intense or fluctuating emotions, and how do these emotions affect your relationships?

In what ways does having a supportive person in your life help you navigate your own emotional highs and lows?

How do you feel about showing your true, unfiltered self to someone? What challenges or benefits do you associate with being completely authentic in a relationship?

12. Love is a Volcano

Love is like a math equation—
Most struggle to solve it,
Gazing at life's chalkboard,
Tracing lines of confusion,
As hearts tangle like forgotten threads.
Some call it calculation or manipulation,
Using formulas of psychology
To extract what they need from a bond,
As if love could be measured
By the balance of the heart.
Yet, love is simple—
Like counting stars at dusk,
Just let the numbers fall,
And the answers will light the dark.

In its purest form, love is reaction—
A volcano of raw emotion,
Erupting beyond control,
Fierce, uncontained,
And always beyond our grasp.

The poem uses the metaphor of a volcanic eruption to explore the nature of love as an intense, uncontrollable force. The poem begins by comparing love to a challenging math equation, illustrating how people often over complicate relationships through manipulation and psychological tactics. It contrasts this complexity with the simplicity of love, likened to counting stars at dusk, suggesting that true understanding comes from allowing love to unfold naturally. The poem concludes with the imagery of a volcanic eruption, emphasizing that love, in its purest form, is a powerful and inevitable chemical reaction that neither reason nor effort can contain. The vivid imagery and metaphors create a dynamic portrayal of love as both a profound and elemental experience.

Reflective Questions:

In what ways have you tried to "solve" love like a math equation in your own life?

How have you experienced love as a raw, uncontrollable force, like a volcano erupting?

Are you allowing love to "unfold naturally," or do you

find yourself trying to manipulate or control the outcome?

13. Smother

Yes, I plead guilty.
I smothered him to death.
No, not with a pillow—
something far heavier.
I watched him writhe,
heard him gasp for air,
but still, I clung tighter,
sure that I knew best.
Others tried to stifle him,
but none could do what I did.
I squeezed harder,
closer than even his mother,
until there was nothing left to give.

Why, you ask?
Because I could.

But no matter how tight I held,
he slipped through my grasp—
too far gone,

too suffocated to breathe.
It wasn't neglect,
or anger that took him.
No—he didn't die.
My love died,
because I buried him
under all of mine.

Description:

This poem explores the destructive power of overwhelming love. The speaker confesses to metaphorically smothering their partner, not with physical force but with emotional intensity and possessiveness. As the relationship unravels, the speaker realizes that their suffocating love, though well-intended, ultimately caused the death of the bond they cherished.

Reflective Questions:

In what ways do you hold on too tightly to people or situations in your life, and how might this affect the relationships you value?

How do your intentions, even when they come from a place of love, sometimes lead to unintentional harm or control over others?

What fears or insecurities drive you to over-give or
smother those you care about, and how can you begin to
release these tendencies?

14. Stress Tick

Gnawing through tender skin,
Like a worm in a rotting apple,
The tick latches, silent and still.

Its victim, unaware, wanders on,
As the tick burrows deeper, unnoticed,
Spreading sickness slow and sure,
Till death whispers in the dark.

Ticks are deadly,
So are our minds.

Circling the same dark thoughts,
Like a hammer driving a nail,
The mind wounds itself, deeper and deeper.

Its prey, oblivious, carries on,
While the mind festers, rotting within,
Till sickness swallows the light.
Till death grips tight.

Stress is the silent killer—
Beware the creeping tick of the mind.

Description:

This poem draws a chilling parallel between a tick and the human mind. It explores how both can quietly latch onto their host, causing damage without being noticed until it's too late. The poem highlights how stress, much like a deadly tick, can silently infiltrate our lives, leading to mental decay and, ultimately, destruction. The imagery of a tick and the hammering thoughts reveal the subtle but profound danger of unchecked stress and overthinking.

Reflective Questions:

In what ways do you allow stress or repetitive thoughts to "latch onto" your mind without noticing their harmful effects? Reflect on moments when you might have ignored early signs of mental strain or stress.

How do you cope when stress or anxiety begins to burrow deeper into your mind? Consider how these feelings manifest in your life and whether you actively address them or let them linger, much like the unnoticed tick.

What repetitive thoughts or fears have taken root in your mind that might be silently draining your emotional and mental health?

15. Chilled Silence

Speak, you beg of me.
But some words are not worth the cost.
I won't splinter my sanity
for a fleeting moment's exchange.

Control is a myth we clutch,
our words are ours to wield.
Yet they chill like iron chains,
damning, hollow, and unbearable.

What becomes of a soul
when words lose their weight?
No truth in their echoes,
no mirror in their steps.

So I linger,
until the truth burns my throat.
A revelation too sharp to utter,
yet cold enough to guard my fraying soul.

Silence enfolds me—
it's armor, it's strength.
Never deadly, but this void,
this absence of truth, chills deeper than any word could.

Description:

This poem explores the tension between speaking and remaining silent, emphasizing the power of unspoken words. The poem reflects on how words, when not carefully chosen, can be burdensome and hollow, while silence serves as a protective and powerful shield. Through vivid imagery and metaphors, it conveys the struggle of guarding one's true thoughts and emotions, and the chilling impact of the void left by unexpressed truths.

Reflective Questions:

What unspoken thoughts or feelings are you currently holding back, and how do they impact your sense of self and your relationships?

In what situations do you use silence as a defense mechanism, and what are you trying to protect yourself from?

How do you reconcile the difference between your inner truths and the words you choose to express outwardly?

16. Barbarian Joker

You shout, your fist slams against the table,
Demanding I agree—
As if my own thoughts hold no weight.

You never seem to understand.
When I say I'm tired,
It's because I've outgrown your childish games.

You throw a name at me,
Sharp and cruel,
Then claim it wasn't meant to wound.

But my anger flares.
You call me a wench,
A foolish little witch.

I clench my fists—
As if I need permission to feel rage.
You dismiss my fury as nothing,
Mocking my words.

You're reckless, relentless,
Too much—
And I beg you to stop,
But you laugh,
Calling me no fun.

When I cry, you belittle my tears,
You say they mean nothing to you—
That I'm weak.

You know exactly where it hurts,
The tender places I hide,
Yet you strike like a snake without restraint.

There's no love here,
I wonder if there ever was.
This relationship,
A cruel joke.

**You're the barbarian Joker,
And me?
I'm the witch you've wrecked.**

Description:

This poem portrays an emotionally abusive relationship,

where one partner uses manipulation, cruelty, and mockery to assert control over the other. The speaker expresses their frustration, anger, and emotional exhaustion from constantly being belittled and verbally attacked. The imagery of fists, sharp words, and a snake's strike highlights the relentless aggression they endure. The speaker questions whether love ever existed in the relationship, feeling reduced to a "witch" wrecked by the "barbarian Joker," symbolizing the emotional chaos inflicted upon them.

Reflective Questions:

In what ways have you allowed someone else to belittle or dismiss your emotions?

Do you find yourself holding back your anger or true feelings out of fear of confrontation?

Are there unresolved patterns of control or manipulation in your relationships that mirror the dynamics in this poem?

17. Soul Steer

We steer our fate,
No command but our own to follow.
Is Fate from God, or ours to hold?
With free will, we choose our way,
Turning from the knocks at our door.

Regret may find us—or perhaps not,
Such is the heart of the human story.
But to accept all as Fate's decree
Is to live without question or wonder.

Without questions, there is no reflection.
Without reflection, how can we know
What we truly desire?
In the end, we settle for Fate,

Calling it God's design—
Yet we, too, are His design,
And within that truth,
We find our freedom.

Discrimination:

This poem reimagines Winston Churchill's famous quote, "We are the masters of our own fate," by exploring the balance between destiny and free will. It challenges the idea that everything in life is predetermined by God's design, suggesting instead that free will grants us the power to shape our own path. Through introspection and self-reflection, the poem urges us not to passively accept everything as fate, but to recognize that we have the spiritual and personal agency to make choices that define our journey. In doing so, we find freedom within God's design rather than being bound by it. This perspective encourages an active engagement with life, steering our soul with intention rather than settling for what appears to be inevitable.

Reflective Questions:

In what areas of your life have you accepted things as "fate" rather than taking control of your choices? How might reclaiming your agency change your path?

Are there desires or ambitions you've suppressed because you believed they weren't aligned with your "destiny"? How can you begin to honor those desires now?

What fears or beliefs keep you from questioning the status quo? How can embracing self-reflection help you uncover hidden truths about your personal power?

18. Unloved

I never knew
Why her pain ran so deep—
It clung to her, day after day.

I couldn't change a thing,
Only watched as she stumbled,
Repeating the same mistakes.

"What's wrong now?"
The weight of too many troubles
Bore down on her fragile frame.

She wandered, lost—
Searching for a place
To feel safe,
A home that never came.

No arms ever reached for her,
No one willing to bear the burden,
Her heart deemed too heavy to hold.

What does one do when they're cast out,
Left to face the cold world alone?
The child once clung to her mother,
But even that grip was pried away.

Thrown into a life of indifference,
Where no one took her hand—
Not out of hate,
But something colder,
Apathy that sealed her fate.

For it's not hatred that destroys,
But indifference—the true opposite of love.
And so, she faded away,
A quiet end, unnoticed,
While the world went on,
Too busy to care.

Description:

This poem delves into the profound pain of a girl rejected by society, illustrating her relentless struggle and ultimate isolation. The poem captures her endless search for safety and acceptance, only to face a world indifferent to her suffering. The powerful imagery conveys her loneliness and the harsh reality of being deemed too burdensome to help. Echoing Elie Wiesel's insight that "the opposite of love is not hate, it's indifference," the poem poignantly illustrates how apathy, rather than hatred, sealed her fate, leading to a quiet, unnoticed end.

Reflective Questions:

In what areas of your life have you felt rejected or unloved, and how has this experience shaped your understanding of your worth? How can acknowledging and confronting these feelings help you heal?

How do you respond to those around you who are struggling or perceived as burdensome? Are there ways you might be inadvertently contributing to their isolation or suffering?

What emotions or beliefs do you have about indifference versus active hatred? How can exploring these concepts help you understand your own responses to others' pain and your capacity for empathy?

19. Shared Path

I never sought a mentor,
Not because I didn't need one—
God knows I stumbled through.
But a mentor?
That meant someone tethered to my struggle,
And I couldn't bear the weight of that,
Didn't need anyone pulling me along.
I thought I was fine on my own.

A mentor walks in shadows,
Not quite a friend,
Older, wiser,
Thinking they hold the map.
But I never needed a guide—
We all leave footprints on the same shore, don't we?

But that doesn't mean I don't listen.
I take in every word,
Internalize their steps,
Admiring their beautifully broken path.

A friend is the quiet mentor,
No pressure, only presence.
Lighting the way softly,
Nurturing growth in firm, yet gentle, words.

But to force a mentor?
It unravels the journey.
The weight of that title—
Too heavy for them, too tight for me.

The best guide is a friend,
With clear lines between us,
Walking beside you,
Not in your shoes, but alongside,
Like two sets of footprints in the sand—
Separate, but always near.

Description:

This poem explores the speaker's reluctance to accept a mentor, reflecting on the delicate balance between guidance and independence. Using the metaphor of footprints in the sand, it highlights the value of a friend as an unpressured, equal companion who walks alongside rather than leading or controlling. The poem contrasts the heavy burden of formal mentorship with the natural, nurturing role of a true friend, emphasizing personal growth without the weight of labels.

Reflective Questions:

In what areas of your life do you resist guidance or support from others, and why do you feel the need to handle those struggles alone?

Reflect on a time when you allowed someone to walk alongside you. How did that connection shape your growth, and what did you learn about trust and vulnerability?

What inner fears or beliefs cause you to view mentorship or asking for help as a burden, and how might you begin to release those perceptions?

20. Our Song

How could a song that made my heart soar,
Light and free, in love with joyous glee,
Now bring me tears by its second chord,
Before the lyrics even start to breathe?

The song you sent me when we were new,
A world of chances that never came true.
It sang of golden colors and the world in your eyes,
But now you don't want me in your life.

A bitter sting, giving pieces of me,
What was it about me you couldn't see?
The song fades out, its meaning now gone,
A reminder of a time I felt like I belonged.

I glance at my face in the car's dim mirror,
Eyes red, streaked with tears, drawing nearer.
My heart aches, wondering if you recall
The day you gave me our song at all.

As I replay the song, it's a bittersweet dance,
A memory of a time we took a chance.
I wonder if the lyrics still hold your heart,
Or if they've drifted away, like we did from the start.

The final chords linger, heavy and clear,
A mournful reminder of love we held dear.
I close my eyes, hoping you might see,
It was a better place when you came along.

Description:

This poignant poem reflects on the transformative power of music in a relationship. Initially a source of joy and hope, the song now evokes sadness and loss as the relationship deteriorates. It speaks to the bittersweet memories attached to a once-beloved song, now tainted by heartbreak and longing. The narrator wrestles with feelings of betrayal and reminiscence, wondering if their former partner shares the same memories of their shared song. Through vivid imagery and raw emotion, the poem captures the ache of nostalgia and the complexities of love lost.

Reflective Questions:

How do you process the emotions tied to certain

memories, and why do they shift from joy to pain over time?

What parts of yourself have you given away in past relationships, and how do you reclaim those pieces without judgment or regret?

Are you holding on to past experiences that no longer serve you, and how can you begin to let go of the pain while still honoring the lessons learned?

21. The Last Embrace

You live two lives: the first unfolds at birth,
The second begins when you grasp
That you hold only one to cherish.

This might be your final existence,
The last poem you ever read,
The final sunrise or sunset you witness.
Is this the end of the journey?

You never know when the end will arrive.
The final moments may not always shine,
But let's make them brimming with meaning,
Filled with tranquility.

If this is the last act of anything,
Let it be done with purpose.
If there is a higher power,
May it be honored through your choices.

Find serenity in your heart,

For one day you will not wake;
Your heart will fall silent.

Revel in fleeting joys,
In adventures embraced,
In places explored,
In lives touched.

Leave a gentle imprint,
For sometimes a soft touch is best.
You need not be overwhelming.

Cherish every breath,
Treasure each friend,
And release the burden of foes.

Description:

This poem explores the profound awareness that life is finite and encourages readers to live fully in every fleeting moment. Through evocative imagery and a contemplative tone, the poem reflects on the significance of our final experiences and the importance of finding peace, purpose, and joy in the present. It serves as a reminder to cherish each breath, embrace every opportunity, and leave a gentle, meaningful mark on the world.

Reflective Questions:

How does recognizing the finite nature of life influence the way you approach your daily choices and interactions?

What are some ways you can find peace and meaning in your everyday experiences, especially knowing that they might be the last of their kind?

In what ways can you leave a positive and gentle impact on others, and how can you release negativity or unresolved conflicts in your life?